THE ABSOLUTELY ANIMAL-FREE COOKBOOK

THE ABSOLUTELY ANIMAL-FREE COOKBOOK

Wendy Turner

Illustrated by Michael Avery

The Book Guild Ltd
Sussex, England

The Book Guild Ltd
25 High Street,
Lewes, Sussex

First published 1997

© Wendy Turner 1997

Set in Times

Typesetting by
Raven Typesetters, Chester, Cheshire

Printed in Great Britain by
Bookcraft (Bath) Ltd, Avon

A catalogue record for this book is
available from the British Library

ISBN 1 85776 268 1

Contents

Main Courses

With thanks to:
Jean Turner, René Carter, Ceri Glen, Helen Tomlinson, Arthur Walker, The Vegan Society and PETA (People for the Ethical Treatment of Animals).

Introduction

An Absolutely Animal-Free diet is one step on from being vegetarian. To be a vegan means not eating meat, fish, dairy products or eggs, in fact anything that has an animal origin. (Of course this means that you don't *wear* animal products either.)

Food is important to us all. It is the basis of many social occasions and a source of comfort, warmth and, of course, nutrition. If it is interesting, tasty and fun it can be a delicious challenge, a fascinating pursuit, a tantalizing team effort: the highlight of the day. It can also be Absolutely Animal-Free.

So why become a vegan, why give up what comprises the majority of the foods we eat? There are many reasons. Some cannot bring themselves to financially support intensive fishing and farming methods which cause pain and suffering to countless animals every year, and deplete the oceans' fish stocks irreparably. Some cannot understand the logic which tells us to love, pet and respect some animals, but kill, eat and mistreat others. Some find the irrational preference for animal farming ecologically, and economically un-sound; for others it is simply a question of health.

Whatever your reasons, all vegans are left with the same question of how to maintain an animal-free diet that *is* interesting, tasty and fun.

When I told a particular friend that I was giving up dairy products and eggs as well as meat and fish, he asked 'But what on earth are you going to eat . . . curried ice cubes?' Rest assured, eating an Absolutely Animal-Free diet does not mean a life sentence of lentil soup and salad, it can be as versatile and as impressive as any other cuisine. The aim of this book is to dispel the myth that we need animal products to create mouthwatering meals. With time and tastebuds, ideas and inspiration from friends and family, I hope that I have compiled a selection of recipes which are quick, simple and based on ingredients which are as readily available as a tin of beans, absolutely animal-free and absolutely delicious!

The concerns of vegans are issues that affect us all. But don't take my word for it! Listed below are two organisations who will be more than happy to give you information on animal farming and its alternatives:

The Vegan Society
Donald Watson House
7 Battle Road
St Leonards-on-Sea
East Sussex
TN37 7AA

Telephone 01424 427393
Facsimile 01424 717064

The Vegan Society promotes diets and ways of living free of all animal products for the benefit of people, animals and the environment. It also publishes the *Animal Free Shopper* — an indispensable guide to vegan products. For an information pack please send two first class stamps.

PETA
People for the Ethical Treatment of Animals
PO Box 3196
London
SW15 3ZG

Founded in 1980 in the United States, PETA are the largest animal rights organisation in the world. PETA's campaigns target animal abuse in laboratories, in the fur trade and meat trades and in the entertainment industry. With nearly 500,000 members worldwide they are at the forefront of the international animal rights movement.

Become Absolutely Animal-Free and you can . . .

- avoid that embarrassing question, 'If you don't eat meat, why do you wear leather?'

- put hours on your shopping time by reading through the list of ingredients on every product in the shop.

- eat Fry's Chocolate Cream smugly as your friends cry out, 'But you can't eat chocolate, you're vegan!'

- endure the meat eater who ruins a meal out by insisting on having a round table discussion about the rights and wrongs of being vegan.

- wear vegetarian Dr Martens and prove that you can be animal free *and* fashionable.

- do a grand tour of your local chip shops asking them which oil they use, then sample the products of all those who give the animal-free answer.

- rest assured that your actions are making a difference.

- watch *Babe* and cry with a clear conscience.

Ten Things that Vegans Get Used to Hearing

- It must be so *difficult* being a vegan.

- But what on earth do you eat?

- Chef says he can do you a plate of vegetables . . .

- Oh the mushroom soup's all right, madam. It's only got a bit of chicken stock in it.

- I'm a vegetarian. I only eat fish.

- But if we didn't breed these animals to eat them they'd be extinct.

- What do you fancy? I think they do salad here . . .

- But sheep need to have their coats sheared . . . don't they?

- I don't suppose you can eat out, being a vegan.

- If you don't milk a cow it will die!

- Mmm, you look very healthy – for a vegan.

Glossary of Ingredients

As the vegan diet is restricted to Absolutely Animal-Free produce, the creative vegan cook has to seek out new ingredients to add flavour, texture and nutrition. Luckily supermarkets and not just health shops now stock vegan products, and the range of Soya substitutes is growing. Here are some ingredients which may not be familiar, as well as some useful information about some that are.

Alcohol

As a general rule, beers and wines are often clarified (cleared) using isinglass (fish swim bladder). Organic wines tend to be animal friendly. Croft sherries are, as well as most ciders. The production of spirits does not appear to involve the use of animal substances. To be on the safe side refer to the Vegan Society's *Animal Free Shopper!*

Beans/Peas

Dried pulses are another great source of protein and flavour, however, if you can't be bothered soaking and boiling them, the tinned varieties are convenient and supermarkets seem to be stocking an ever increasing selection. They are basically interchangeable, so experimentation is the name of the game.

Cream cheese

Sometimes difficult to obtain, but it can be found in most healthfood shops.

Curry paste

There are many brands on offer, they are a great short cut to an authentic taste, but be warned, many contain animal products, particularly Thai pastes which contain fish sauces and shrimp.

Herbs and Spices

In a perfect world, all herbs would be fresh, and all spices freshly ground. Use them when you can, however, there are some very good freeze-dried herbs, and some preserved in oil, which are a quick alternative.

Jelly
Made by Just Wholefoods and Snowcrest. Available from healthfood shops.

Marmite
The well-known spread, great on toast, but also a good provider of flavour and vitamins.

Mushrooms
Mushrooms come in an astonishing array of varieties. Delicious and exotic wild mushrooms like chanterelle, cep and porchino are harvested from forests and fields throughout Europe and are available fresh or dried. Although fresh are more convenient, do not be put off the dried varieties. They are cheaper, you can use them as required and they have a richer, nuttier flavour. Farmed Chinese or Shi'Take mushrooms are also available fresh or dried, they have a less powerful but distinctively oriental flavour. The attractive Oyster mushroom is also farmed and readily available from supermarkets. These fabulous fungi do not, however, detract from the humble field, chestnut and button mushrooms which are every bit as tasty and great absorbers of flavours. Farmed mushrooms should be wiped or peeled, but always wash wild mushrooms, even the dried ones, they often contain bits of forest, and *never* pick your own unless you are an expert, some toadstools can kill.

Nuts
The nut is another vegan life saver, full of protein *and* taste, nuts keep indefinitely, and can be used instead of meat in a variety of ways.

Oils
For some, oils are a means to an end; the medium for their fried foods. But oils are a fascinating and flavourful addition to any larder. Sunflower and peanut oils are good for frying, olive oils for salad dressings, but don't forget the nutty flavours of walnut, hazelnut and sesame seed oils, which add zing to stir fries and salads, and the many flavoured oils which are now available: chilli, herb, and lemon.

Pasta, wheat
Not all pasta is vegan! Some dried pasta varieties have egg in them to bind them, unfortunately most fresh pasta does too. It is always worth checking.

Pastry
Frozen pastry is a godsend. Puff pastry, paper thin filo and short crust can be bought from most supermarkets. However some contain animal fat, so checking the label is essential.

Rice

There are many sorts of rice, and the right type should be used for each of its many applications. Long grain (easy cook) is a staple accompaniment; basmati, a fragrant addition to any oriental food; Italian rice, notably shorter and rounder, is the ideal basis for risotto, sticky and robust.

Rice Milk

Rice Dream and Lima's Rev Riz are readily available in most healthfood shops.

Soy sauce

Made from fermented Soya beans, this is a rich and fragrant addition to any meal, oriental or not. It comes in varying strengths from light to dark and the Japanese variety is particularly full-flavoured.

Soya Cream

Available from Tesco, Sainsbury and Safeway.

Soya ice cream

Swedish Glace (in a variety of flavours) is available from healthfood shops, and most of the major supermarkets. Other brands may be found in healthfood shops.

Soya margarine

Most margarines contain dairy products and vitamin D_3 (derived from fish oil or sheep wool fat). Vegan margarines include Safeway's Soya, Sainsbury's Soya, Suma Wholefoods' Soya and Sunflower and Fresh Fields Pure Sunflower.

Soya 'Milk'

Thanks to the EU it is now illegal for producers to refer to non-dairy alternatives as 'Milk' so look out for the catchy name 'Soya non-dairy alternative to milk' or 'Soya Drink'. Available in all healthfood shops and most supermarkets.

Stock

Good stock is the basis for any great meal, unfortunately, most of us don't bother to have a stock pot bubbling away on the stove. Thankfully the quality of vegetable stock cubes has increased amazingly in recent years, however, it is still worth checking the label for lactose. Buy Vegetarian Oxo, Knorr and Safeway Vegetable Stock with confidence.

Tahini
Made from sesame seeds, this paste resembles peanut butter. It adds a nutty richness to many meals, especially Hummus. Available in dark or light.

Tofu
This is soya bean curd, once a rarity but now available from most supermarkets in plain, smoked and marinated varieties.

Vegan (Hard) Cheese
Available from healthfood shops. Choose from the Redwood Cheezly or Bue Island Food's Scheese ranges.

Whole egg replacer
You should be able to find either Ener-G Egg replacer or Loprofin Egg replacer in your local healthfood shop.

Wine Vinegar
Will not be animal-free if the wine was clarified with isinglass. If in doubt, select from the Martlet brand range or buy Waitrose White Wine Vinegar.

Yeast flakes
Engevita Nutritional Yeast Flakes can be found in Holland and Barratt and most other healthfood shops.

Soups and Starters

Mushroom and Walnut Soup

A subtle oriental soup with a rich, earthy flavour.

2 tablespoons of groundnut oil
110g (4oz) chopped walnuts
450g (16oz) mushrooms, sliced thinly
2 pints of water
4 tablespoons of soy sauce

1. Over a high heat, sauté the walnuts in the oil for 1 minute.
2. Add the mushrooms.
3. Once they have started to lose liquid pour in the water.
4. Bring to the boil then simmer for 10 minutes.
5. Add the soy sauce and serve immediately.

Serves four

20 mins

Watercress Soup

The freshest taste of summer, serve hot or chilled.

1 medium sized onion
2 bunches of watercress
50g (2oz) soya margarine
40g (1½ oz) plain flour
850ml (1½ pints) vegetable stock
250ml (½ pint) soya milk
150ml (¼ pint) soya cream
Seasoning to taste

1. Chop the onion very finely, preferably in a food processor.
2. Chop up the bunches of watercress very finely, including stalks.
3. Melt the soya margarine in a large non-stick pan and fry the onion and watercress over a moderate heat until soft.
4. Add the flour and stir well, then remove from the heat.
5. Stir in the stock and milk gradually.
6. Return to the heat and stir until the soup thickens. Simmer for about 15–20 minutes, making sure that it doesn't boil.
7. Season, and serve immediately with a little swirl of soya cream on top of each helping.

Serves four

40 mins

3

Carrot and Peanut Butter Soup

Organic carrots have a more delicate, sweet flavour. Use them in this recipe for a wholesome fragrance.

2 *tablespoons of sunflower oil*
2 *shallots or small onions, roughly chopped*
170g (6oz) *carrots, roughly diced*
2 *teaspoons of unsweetened peanut butter*
1 *pint of vegetable stock*
Additional water
Salt to taste

1. Over a medium heat fry the onions in the sunflower oil until lightly cooked.
2. Add the carrot and fry for a further 5 minutes
3. Add the peanut butter and the vegetable stock.
4. Bring to the boil, cover and simmer for 20 minutes.
5. Remove from the heat and liquidize.
6. Return to the saucepan and add the water until the soup reaches the desired consistency.
7. Heat through, season to taste and serve immediately.

Taste of Things to Come

One of my first memories of any of our pets was of a tortoise called George. My two sisters had some friends over to play and I was tagging along. After playing in the wigwam, listening to Cliff Richard and then making our dog Pat play the part of the wolf in our version of Little Red Riding Hood, there was suddenly a lull in the proceedings. The day's activities had come to an abrupt end and everyone was trying to think of something fun to do.

'I know,' said Ruth, 'let's bath George!'

'Good idea!' we all cried and set off to the bottom garden to find him. The only trouble was that George was long since dead and in order to put a shine on his shell he had to be dug up from his shallow grave. As I recall this wasn't a one-off pursuit and poor old George must have been the cleanest dead tortoise in Stoke-on-Trent.

So I admit we were pretty revolting, but when it came to animals we also became rather cunning. All the animals we had were strays (even the tortoise had simply wandered into the garden) and none of them were ever acquired on purpose. So how could we get other furry friends when our parents clearly wouldn't buy them for us? Simple, we'd buy the pets for them! This had to be thought out though. Presenting Dad with a gerbil on his birthday would not have the desired reaction and it was felt that Mum would be a more sympathetic and enthusiastic recipient for our living presents. Other mums would get flowers and chocolates on Mothers' Day but ours would get a hamster or a guinea pig complete with food, lodgings and a name.

'It'll have to go!' Dad would shout.

'It's my present,' Mum would fight in reply, 'She's called Snowdrop and she's staying here!'

And so the new pet would settle into his or her new home and Dad would become as attached to it as the rest of us. Being older and wiser, I would now never dream of buying a pet for anyone, even close family, as a surprise present. Pets are for life, not just for Mothers' Day.

Wild Mushroom Paté

Served with hot wholegrain toast, this convenient starter is best made a day in advance.

Serves eight

30 mins + 1 hour

1 large onion, finely chopped
1 small clove garlic, finely chopped
2 tablespoons of olive oil
150 ml (¼ pint) white wine (we used
*   Bordeaux Dry from Asda)*
450g (1lb) assorted fresh wild mushrooms
1 tablespoon of fresh parsley, finely
*   chopped*
1 tablespoon of soya cream
Salt & freshly ground black pepper to taste

1. Slowly soften the garlic and onion in a pan with the olive oil.
2. Add all the other ingredients and cook gently for 10 minutes.
3. Pass through a sieve or liquidize.
4. Place in a ramekin dish, cover and allow to cool.
5. Transfer to the fridge for at least 1 hour before serving.

American Butterbean Paté

A full flavoured, coarse paté to rival any Ardennes.

1 teaspoon of olive oil
2 garlic cloves, crushed
1 onion, 225g (8oz) peeled and minced
50g (2oz) minced carrot
50g (2oz) minced mushrooms
2 tablespoons chopped fresh parsley
1½ cups of cooked butterbeans
1 tablespoon of nutritional yeast flakes
  (available from your local healthfood
  shop)
1 teaspoon of soy sauce

1. Heat the oil in a large pan over a medium to high heat.
2. Sauté the garlic, onion, carrot, mushrooms and parsley for about five minutes until the onion is soft, but not browned.
3. Liquidize the beans, nutritional yeast flakes and soy sauce together until the mixture is smooth.
4. Stir in the sautéed vegetables.
5. Place in a ramekin dish, cover and allow to cool.
6. Transfer to the fridge for at least 1 hour before serving.

Serves eight

20 mins + 1 hour

American Olive Spread

This keeps well in the refrigerator. Spread it on warm Ciabatta or Foccacia and top with a slice of ripe tomato for an instant animal-free snack.

Serves four

5 mins

225g (8oz) *stoned black olives*
3 tablespoons of capers
½ teaspoon of rosemary
½ teaspoon of oregano
50ml (2 fl oz) *olive oil*

Liquidize all the ingredients together for a few seconds to get a coarsely ground up mixture.

Stoned black olives

Wild Mushroom Soup

A quick and exotic treat.

Serves four

30 mins

1 large onion, finely chopped
1 small clove garlic, finely chopped
2 tablespoons of olive oil
300 ml (½ pint) *white wine (we used Bordeaux Dry from Asda)*
450g (1lb) *assorted fresh wild mushrooms*
1 tablespoon of fresh parsley, finely chopped
300 ml (½ pint) *vegetable stock*
Salt & freshly ground black pepper to taste

1. Slowly soften the garlic and onion in a pan with the olive oil.
2. Add all the other ingredients and cook gently for 10 minutes.
3. Pass through a sieve or liquidize.
4. Return to the heat and simmer for 3 minutes. Serve immediately.

Fussy Eater

We used to have a lovely pond in the garden. Well, it still is a lovely pond, it just doesn't have over 150 koi carp in it any more. A hungry heron saw to that a few winters ago. After years of successfully keeping these beautiful fish, a heron swooped down and scoffed the lot! So all the fish had gone, but it was winter, and the heron stood forlornly by the side of the pond, his feathers puffed up against the biting cold, waiting for the fish that never came. Mum witnessed all this from the kitchen window and began to take pity on this proud looking bird who appeared to be on the brink of starvation. And if, indeed, he was starving, she was going to find a way to feed him.

The heron was obviously forgiven for swallowing about a thousand pounds worth of koi as Mum headed down to the Co-op to buy him some fish for his supper. Cod was on the menu and after following the microwave instructions she went down to the pond and positioned the defrosted piece of fish on a large lily pad. Watching from the kitchen, Mum was disappointed to see that the heron was not in the least bit interested. We found out later that they only like to eat live fish and up to press these are not available to buy in Norton village Co-op.

Dips

The dip is a brilliant invention; as a starter it is easy and tasty, with a few drinks it is unrivalled! Dip in with corn nachos, bread sticks or crunchy crudités.

Serves six

15 mins +30 mins

Guacamole Dip

1 small onion, skinned
2 cloves of garlic, skinned
½ inch piece of fresh root ginger, peeled
2 large ripe avocados
finely grated rind and juice of 1 small lime
2 tablespoons of chopped fresh coriander
1 teaspoon of ground coriander
1 teaspoon of ground cumin
½ teaspoon of chilli powder
Salt & freshly ground black pepper to taste

1. Using a food processor and with the machine running, drop the onions, garlic and ginger through the funnel, processing until finely chopped.
2. Peel and stone the avocados then put in the blender with all the remaining ingredients. Process until smooth.
3. Add the salt and pepper to taste.
4. Cover and chill for half an hour before serving.

Serves six

5 mins +30 mins

Bean Dip

225g (8oz) cooked butterbeans
2 tablespoons of olive oil
4 teaspoons of wine vinegar
2 cloves of garlic, crushed

1. Liquidize the butterbeans, adding the garlic, oil and vinegar.
2. Chill before serving.

Hummus

225g (8oz) *cooked chick peas*
2 teaspoons of tahini
2 cloves of garlic, crushed
3 teaspoons of lemon juice
Olive oil

1. Liquidize the chick peas using some water to make a thick puree.
2. Add the tahini, garlic and lemon juice and enough olive oil to make a thick sauce.
3. Chill before serving

Serves six

5 mins
+30 mins

Tomato Dip

455g (1lb) *tomatoes, chopped*
1 clove of garlic, crushed
1 small onion, sliced
1 teaspoon of mixed herbs
1 teaspoon of brown sugar
1 tablespoon of wine vinegar

1. Place the tomatoes and onion in a pan over a gentle heat and add the garlic and herbs.
2. Cook for about 20 minutes until the mixture forms a thick puree, stirring occasionally.
3. Liquidize the mixture and add the vinegar and brown sugar.
4. Return to the heat, bring to the boil, and take off the heat.
5. Serve warm.

Serves six

30 mins

Pineapple Dip

225g (8oz) *fresh pineapple, chopped*
1 large onion, chopped
2 tablespoons of olive oil
1 tablespoon of wine vinegar
1 teaspoon of cinnamon

1. Fry the pineapple and onion in the olive oil until golden brown.
2. Drain and place in a liquidizer with the vinegar and cinnamon, blending to a smooth puree.
3. Chill before serving.

Serves six

10 mins
+30 mins

Having a dip

Vegetable Kebabs with Satay Sauce

Indonesian cuisine predominantly uses seafood and meat for their kebabs. This version keeps the subtle Eastern flavours – but is totally animal-free!

Serves four

2 medium sized potatoes, boiled and cut into 2.5cm/1 inch pieces
1 large yellow pepper, seeded and cut as above
1 aubergine, cut as above
12 button mushrooms, whole
1 medium sized onion, roughly sliced
2 tablespoons of lemon juice
4 tablespoons of olive oil
Seasoning

Serve with Satay Sauce

1. Put the vegetables into a large bowl. Add the olive oil, lemon juice and seasoning to taste. Stand for 15 minutes, gently stirring occasionally.
2. Thread the vegetables as selected on to kebab skewers and brush with the juices remaining in the bowl.
3. Grill, turning at intervals until cooked evenly.

Satay Sauce

100g (4oz) *crunchy peanut butter*
1 tablespoon of olive oil
1 tablespoon of dark soy sauce
2 teaspoons of brown sugar
¼ teaspoon of chilli powder, or to taste
140ml (¼ pint) *coconut milk*
1 tablespoon of lemon juice
2 tablespoons of soya cream

25 mins + 10 mins

1. Put the peanut butter into a bowl. Add the oil, 1 teaspoon of sugar, chilli powder and lemon juice.
2. Add the coconut milk.
3. Mix the rest of the sugar with the soy sauce and add to the mixture.
4. Heat very gently over a low heat in a non-stick pan.
5. Add the soya cream just before serving.

Spring Rolls with Plum Sauce

Delicate Chinese flavours combined in a crisp filo roll with a piquant fruity dip.

Plum Sauce
450g (1lb) jar of stoneless plum jam
300ml (½ pint) of spiced pickling vinegar

1. Using a non-stick pan on a low heat, melt the plum jam.
2. Add the vinegar and cook for about 10 minutes, stirring frequently.
3. Leave to cool and thicken.

Spring roll mixture
225g (8oz) bean sprouts
50g (2oz) mushrooms, finely chopped
125g (4oz) frozen mixed vegetables
1 small onion, finely chopped
1 tablespoon rapeseed or olive oil
3 tablespoons of light soy sauce
1 teaspoon of Marmite
2 teaspoons of cornflour
1 250g (9oz) packet of filo pastry

1. Bring the mixed vegetables to the boil and cook for 3 minutes.
2. In a wok or large pan, stir fry the onion, mushrooms, and mixed vegetables in a little rapeseed oil or olive oil adding the soy sauce and Marmite.
4. Roll out the filo pastry and follow instructions as directed for rolls, making up 8.
5. Bake in a preheated oven at 200°C (400°F) for about 20 minutes or until crisp and golden.

Serves eight

15 mins + 40 mins

13

Main Courses

Carrot Burgers

This animal-free version of the fast food favourite can be served like any other burger. Try it in a toasted seasame bun with soya mayonnaise, gherkin and iceberg lettuce.

4 medium carrots
4 teaspoons of coriander seeds
2 teaspoons of cumin seeds
8 tablespoons of oats
Salt and pepper to taste
Olive oil for frying

1. Scrub and dice the carrots then boil or steam them until tender.
2. Drain and mash thoroughly.
3. Meanwhile roast the coriander and cumin seeds in a dry pan over a medium heat until slightly brown and pungent.
4. Grind the seeds into a dry powder with a mortar and pestle.
5. Add the ground seeds to the mashed carrot and then the oats.
6. Season to taste with salt and pepper and leave to cool.
7. Form into 4 burgers and lightly fry in oil until golden on both sides.

Serves four

40 mins

Scrub and dice the carrots

Wild Mushroom Risotto

A wonderful way to get the most out of the subtle flavour of mushrooms. Try it with fresh Shi'Take or oyster mushrooms. For a special occasion, a selection of wild mushrooms makes this a real treat.

Serves four

30 mins

2 large onions, finely chopped
300g (10oz) arborio rice
Vegetable stock
450g (16oz) assorted mushrooms
4 tablespoons of finely chopped fresh mixed
    herbs, e.g. basil, coriander and parsley
1 tablespoon of olive oil
2 cloves of garlic, crushed
1 glass vegan dry white wine
(we used Cotes de Gascogne from Safeways).

1. Heat the oil in a pan and add the onions and garlic. Heat through until the onions are tender.
2. Add the rice, stirring all the time.
3. When the rice starts to glisten add the wine.
4. Start to add the stock slowly, stirring occasionally. Do not let the rice dry out. Add enough stock to keep it moist – no more and no less.
5. 5–10 minutes later add the mushrooms and 3 tablespoons of the herbs, saving 1 tablespoon of them for garnish.
6. Continue to add the stock as required, stirring occasionally.
7. When the rice is cooked through stop adding liquid. Remove from the heat, cover tightly with a lid and allow to stand for 3 minutes.
8. Remove the lid, sprinkle with the remaining herbs and serve.

Creamy Mushroom and Onion Korma with Cashew Nuts

This is my favourite dish, especially when served with thick chipped potatoes! Also goes well with Pilaw rice.

4 medium onions, sliced
125g (4oz) mushrooms, sliced
50g (2oz) sultanas
40g (1½ oz) roasted cashew nuts
50g (2oz) Patak's Original Korma Curry Paste (use this or any other animal-free brand, available at your local supermarket)
50g (2oz) vegetable ghee
50g(2oz) creamed coconut dissolved in 450ml (¾ pint) of hot water
150ml ((¼ pint) soya cream

1. Melt the vegetable ghee in a large frying pan over a hot heat. Add the onions.
2. Once the onions are browned, add the sultanas and cashew nuts.
3. Add the creamed coconut and water and stir well.
4. Add the sliced mushrooms.
5. Once the liquid has reduced by a quarter, add the curry paste and continue to cook. Now turn down the heat and simmer for 15 minutes.
6. Remove from the heat and add the soya cream. Stir in well and serve immediately.

Serves four

30 mins

Quick and Easy Stuffed Peppers with Rice

Another fast, filling favourite. Add pine nuts, chopped tomatoes and fresh basil for an Italian variation.

2 large red peppers
2 large green peppers
1 packet of frozen vegetable and rice mixture
Soy sauce (optional)

1. Cook the peppers in boiling water for 5 minutes, or until just soft. Cut off the tops and de-seed.
2. Cook the rice as directed on the packet. (When cooked sprinkle with soy sauce if desired.)
3. Stuff the peppers with the rice and replace the lids.
4. Place in a greased shallow oven proof dish and brush the peppers with a little vegan margarine.
5. Place on the top shelf of a pre-heated oven at 180°C (350°F) for 5–7 minutes or until the peppers are tender and the filling is hot.

Serves four

30 mins

Pie in the Sky

Oh, those nerve racking aeroplane journeys! The plane starts to taxi down the runway and your palms start to sweat. The wheels leave the ground and your stomach turns over. The great metal tube soars into the air and now you really are panicking, a totally nervous wreck as you wonder for the zillionth time that morning '*What will they give me to eat?*'

Very few airlines I've flown with appear to know a vegetarian from a librarian and a vegan from a Vulcan. Most have much to learn about special dietary requirements, because rest assured, however much effort you make, however many times you telephone, however many times you try to explain the type of meal you want, they will always sneak something in there which goes against your animal-free principles. You ask for vegan, you ask for meat-free and lactose-free, you try calling it pure vegetarian or completely animal-free. Then you get desperate, and ever so slightly annoyed. How do you get your point across? You want nothing that's been *near* an animal in any shape or form. You want nothing that's come *from* an animal and nothing that's come *out* of an animal. But still the penny hasn't dropped and someone in the catering department is determined to ruin your trip by giving you lactose laden biscuits and the most common offender, milk based margarine. So this is the situation – you've clearly asked for a milk-free meal, yet the margarine packet on your tray clearly has skimmed milk listed in the ingredients. Is the concept of soya margarine so hard to grasp? And it would so help in the consumption of those hard lumps of dough that masquerade as fresh bread.

Is it any wonder that you fall off the plane totally plastered?

'Would you like a drink, madam?' asks the air hostess.

'Yes please, two double vodkas with tonic,' you reply, determined to anaesthetize yourself against the disappointment of the ill considered grub that's been placed before you. The ensuing hangover then gets blamed fairly and squarely on that little tablet of margarine that's now melting away in the bottom of your handbag, because this time, *this* time, you are determined to send it back to the airline with a stinking letter of complaint. Not that this will get you anywhere. It was a mistake, a moment of carelessness, a terrible oversight and of course it won't happen again ... and er, sorry madam, but what exactly is a vegan?

Cheesy Stuffed Peppers

The stuffing gives a lovely nutty and cheesy taste and makes a delicious filling for jacket potatoes.

4 large or **6** medium peppers (any colour or a mixture)
Stuffing:-
1 large onion, finely chopped
1 celery stick, finely chopped
25g (1oz) soya margarine
125g (4oz) mushrooms, thinly sliced
50g (2oz) hard vegan cheese grated and mixed with ¼ teaspoon of mustard
1 tablespoon of tomato puree
125g (4oz) mixed chopped nuts
½ teaspoon of cinnamon
½ teaspoon of rosemary
75g (3oz) fresh breadcrumbs
Equivalent of 1 egg replacer made up as directed on the packet (check the product for non-animal content)

1. Mix the stuffing ingredients together and reserve.
2. Cook the peppers in boiling water for 5 minutes or until just soft. Cut off the tops and de-seed.
3. Stuff the peppers with the mixture and replace the lids.
4. Place in a greased shallow oven proof dish and brush the peppers with a little soya margarine.
5. Bake on the top shelf of a pre-heated oven at 180°C (350°F) for 20 minutes or until the peppers are tender and the filling is hot.

Fridge Pie with Nut Pastry

An ideal recipe for using up all those left-over vegetables that lurk in the fridge before you finally decide that they look too tired and unappetising to do anything with!

Serves four

675g (1½lb) cooked mixed vegetables, e.g. broccoli, sliced potatoes, carrots, peas etc. In fact any appropriate 'left over' vegetables in the fridge!
2 tablespoons of rapeseed oil
1 large onion, sliced
25g (1oz) soya margarine
25g (1oz) flour
300ml (½ pint) vegetable stock
Marmite to taste

Pastry
250g (9oz) self-raising flour
125g (4oz) hard vegetable fat (e.g. Trex)
75g (3oz) mixed ground nuts, e.g. brazil, hazel and walnuts
4 tablespoons of water to mix

45 mins

1. Fry the onion in the oil.
2. Melt the soya margarine in a roomy pan.
3. Stir in the flour and add vegetable stock gradually.
4. Stir in a teaspoon or more Marmite to taste.
5. Add to the onion and vegetables, but put together gently so as not to destroy their shape.
6. Turn out into a baking dish.
7. Make the nut pastry. Sieve the flour. Add the Trex and rub into the flour until the mixture looks like fine breadcrumbs. Add the nuts. Add the water to form a dough. Roll out onto a floured surface and cover the vegetables in the dish.
8. Bake in a pre-heated oven at 220°C (424°F) for about 30 minutes or until the filling is hot and the pastry is golden.

Left-over vegetables, too tired and unappetising to do anything with

Exotic Vegetable Pie

Fragrant and fresh, this pie is delicious with minted new potatoes and salad in summer, or with mash in winter.

15 very small whole mushrooms
1 green pepper, de-seeded and sliced into
*   about 8 pieces*
1 red or yellow pepper, prepared as above
2 courgettes trimmed and sliced into rings
1 large aubergine sliced into rings
3 cloves of garlic, sliced
4½ tablespoons of olive oil
4 tablespoons of balsamic vinegar
450g (1lb) bought puff pastry

1. Place all the vegetables on a large baking tray. Drizzle the oil and the vinegar over them.
2. Place in a pre-heated oven at 200°C (400°F) for about 20 minutes until they are tender.
3. Remove and increase the oven temperature to 220°C (420°F).
4. Roll out the pastry and line a shallow pie dish. Fill with the vegetable mixture and cover with a pastry lid.
5. Bake for about 25–30 minutes or until the pastry is well risen and golden brown. Serve immediately.

If you prefer to make your own pastry, try the following recipe:

225g (8oz) self-raising flour
125g (4oz) vegetable fat
4 tablespoons water to mix

Sieve the flour. Add the fat and rub into the flour until the mixture looks like fine bread crumbs. Add enough cold water to form a dough. Roll out on a floured surface.

If using Trex follow the recipe on the packet as the proportion of flour to fat is different, i.e.
280g (10 oz) flour
125g (4oz) Trex

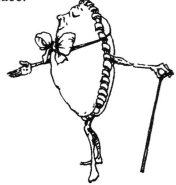

Serves four

1 hour

Stir Fried Tofu with Oyster Mushrooms and Spring Onions

Tofu is extremely versatile and is excellent at absorbing different flavours. For a quick and easy variation try the smoked or ready marinated versions.

Serves four

30 mins

450g (16oz) tofu, diced (available from supermarkets or your local health food shop)
2 teaspoons of soy sauce
Juice of **2** lemons
2 teaspoons of sesame oil
2 tablespoons of sunflower oil
16 spring onions, sliced
2 cloves of garlic, crushed
225g (8oz) oyster mushrooms, torn
Salt and pepper to taste

1. Toss the tofu in a bowl with the soy sauce, juice from one lemon and pepper to taste.
2. Heat the oils in a wok over a moderate to high heat, adding the garlic and sliced spring onions. Stir fry for 1 or 2 minutes.
3. Drain the tofu, reserving the liquid, and add to the wok. Stir fry for a further 1 minute.
4. Add the liquid and stir fry for a further minute.
5. Add the mushrooms and stir fry for 2 minutes.
6. Add salt and pepper to taste and sprinkle the remaining lemon juice over.

Serve with Chinese wheat noodles or rice.

24

Mushroom and Soy Pie

An excellent dish to play about with – try adding onions and ready marinated tofu pieces to the mushrooms.

325g (12oz) breakfast mushrooms, roughly
    chopped
2 tablespoons of sunflower oil
2 tablespoons of soy sauce
450g (1lb) old potatoes
25g (1oz) soya margarine
Salt and pepper to taste

1. Boil the potatoes then mash well with the margarine, salt and pepper.
2. Over a high heat sauté the mushrooms for 1 minute.
3. Cover and turn down the heat. Sweat the mushrooms until at least a tablespoon of juice has come out.
4. Add the soy sauce and pour the mushrooms and juices into an oven proof dish.
5. Cover with the mashed potatoes and dot the top with some soya margarine.
6. Place in a pre-heated oven at 220°C (425°F) for 20 minutes or until the potato is brown and crisp.

Serves four

35 mins

Sweat the mushrooms

Extra Dough

Presenting the second series of Absolutely Animals was the first time I had filmed with our furry friends, that is if you discount working with News Bunny on *Live TV*. But it wasn't the first time I had *tried* to film with animals. That happened a couple of years before, when as a freelance writer and eager for extra cash, my boyfriend and I made a shameless attempt to get £250 from Jeremy Beadle's programme, *You've Been Framed*.

We were feeding my two ponies one night when one of them, Caramac, gave us the idea for the money raising scam. I was bending over the feed bin, bottom in the air, when Caramac came up behind me, put his head between my legs and tossed me head first into a vat of rolled barley. Convinced that he would do it again if given the chance we borrowed a camcorder and set up the whole thing once more. But was he interested in raising my bank balance? No, he wasn't, and no amount of standing over the feed bin, legs apart with a carrot as a bribe would make him repeat the trick. Nowadays I know better than to expect any animal to perform for the cameras. It's quite true – you can lead a horse to water but you can't make him push you in.

Oven Pizza with Roast Vegetable Topping

The full flavour of roasted vegetables makes the usual addition of cheese superfluous on this pizza. However, die-hard traditionalists can top the vegetables with grated vegan cheese before serving.

Base
250g (10oz) self-raising flour, sieved
25g (1oz) soya margarine
½ level tablespoon of mixed dried herbs
A pinch of dry mustard
Water to mix

1. Put the flour and margarine in a bowl.
2. Rub the margarine into the flour as for pastry.
3. Add the herbs and mustard.
4. Make a well in the middle and add the water gradually. Mix to form a dough, handling lightly as for pastry.
5. Divide the dough into 4 pieces and roll each piece out on a floured board forming into disc shapes about 20cm (8 inches) across.
6. Cook in a hot oven at 220°C (425°F) for 20 minutes. Put to one side and make the topping.

Topping
1 large aubergine, topped and tailed and cut into rings
2 medium courgettes, topped and tailed and cut into wedges
1 large yellow pepper, de-seeded and cut into slices
2 medium heads of fennel, sliced
1 large onion sliced
225g (½lb) button mushrooms, whole
225g (½lb) cherry tomatoes
1 tablespoon of balsamic vinegar
5 tablespoons of dark soy sauce
5 tablespoons of rapeseed oil

1. Heat 4 tablespoons of the oil in a large roasting tin for about 4 minutes or until it is hot, on the middle shelf of a pre-heated oven at 220°C (425°F).
2. Add all the vegetables apart from the tomatoes.
3. Cook for 35 minutes then add the tomatoes. Drizzle the remaining oil, the vinegar and soy sauce over the vegetables and stir gently. Cook for a further 15 minutes.
4. Place the pizza bases in the oven to heat through just a few minutes before the vegetables are ready.
5. Divide the roasted vegetables between the 4 hot pizza bases and serve immediately.

Serves four

*30 mins
+
40 mins*

Chilli Con 'Carne'

This is a spicy dish, full of flavour and ideal with rice or jacket potatoes, and a crisp green salad.

Ingredients 'A'

2 medium onions, finely chopped
2 cloves of garlic, finely chopped
1 stick of celery, finely chopped
1 green pepper, de-seeded and finely chopped
1 green chilli, de-seeded and finely chopped
1 red (extra hot) chilli, de-seeded and
    finely chopped
1 teaspoon of cumin powder
2 tablespoons of olive oil
1 level teaspoon of sugar
2 tins of chopped tomatoes
2 generous glasses red wine
(we used a Beaujolais Villages from
    Marks and Spencer.)

1. Using a large saucepan, start by gently frying the onions, garlic and celery in the olive oil.
2. Add all the rest of the ingredients 'A'.
3. Cook for approximately 20 minutes, stirring occasionally.
4. Now add the kidney beans and the soya mince and cook for a further 10 minutes.

Ingredients 'B'

2 tins of kidney beans, drained
275g (10oz) soya mince hydrated in 750ml
(1¼ pints) of water. (Hydrate in the

microwave for about 15 minutes or until tender.) Soya mince may also be bought frozen and ready for use.

Fakes and Fools

Some vegans and vegetarians simply don't like the taste of meat, and then there are those that do, but have given it up for moral reasons. I happen to like the meat substitutes you can buy, some of which are so convincing that many a meat eater can't tell them from the real thing. At the end of the day it's each to his own. If you don't like meat full stop then that's fine, but if you like the animal-free meat substitutes then eat them and enjoy. Fake products are constantly proving that we don't need to use and abuse animals, either for our stomachs or for our vanity. So the moral of this story? Eat and wear fakes and be proud of it.

Pasta in Cream Cheese Sauce

This is great served with sautéed leeks or grilled aubergines.

Serves four

400g (14oz) *Tagliatelle pasta*
4 *medium onions, sliced*
150g (6oz) *animal-free cream cheese (available from your local health food shop)*
150ml (¼ pint) *soya milk*
2 *cloves of garlic, crushed*
50g (2oz) *soya margarine*
2 *tablespoons of olive oil*
2 *tablespoons of basil and coriander, finely chopped*
Parsley to garnish

30 mins

1. Cook enough pasta for four in boiling salted water until 'al dente'. Remove from heat, drain and cover.
2. Heat the olive oil in a large saucepan.
3. Add the sliced onion and crushed garlic cloves. Allow to sweat gently, but do not brown.
4. Remove the onions and place to one side. Melt the margarine in the same pan then add the soya milk and stir in the cream cheese.
5. Add the basil and coriander.
6. Stir gently until heated through, then add the cooked onions. Do not let the mixture get too thick and add more soya milk if needed to reach a 'coating back of spoon' consistency.
7. Add the cooked pasta and heat through.
8. Sprinkle with chopped parsley and serve immediately.

'Beef' and Stout Pie

Traditional pub grub with a conscience – great for cold winter nights accompanied by mashed seasonal root vegetables with a sprinkle of nutmeg.

175g (6oz) *beef flavoured soya chunks hydrated in 750ml (1¼ pints) of water. (Hydrate in the microwave for about 10 minutes or until tender). Soya chunks are available from your local health food shop*

1 *tablespoon of rapeseed oil*

1 *large onion, peeled and sliced*

2 *tablespoons of fresh chopped parsley*

1 *pint of stock – Marmite stock cubes or vegetarian Oxo cubes*

250ml (8fl oz) *Stout (we used Carlsberg Tetley Alloa Sweet Stout.)*

75g (3oz) *button mushrooms, halved*

225g (8oz) *bought puff pastry*

1. Make up the stock and stir in the soya chunks.
2. Add the stout.
3. Heat the oil and fry the onions until tender and golden then add the parsley and mushrooms.
4. Mix all ingredients together and spoon into a pie dish and cover with the rolled out pastry.
5. Cook in a pre-heated oven at 220°C (475°F) for about 30 minutes or until the pastry is golden and well risen.

Serves four

45 mins

31

Out to Lunch

'But where do you find any food you can eat?' people ask when they learn about your animal-free diet. And once again you explain that everything you eat really can be found here on planet earth and better than that, you can find it easily in your local high street. Apart from egg free mayonnaise, mock bacon rashers and marinated tofu pieces, it is quite amazing what the average high street can become home to. Take Middlesbrough high street for example, an ordinary kind of place which one lunchtime had an extraordinary kind of visitor, a terrapin to be exact, a lost and lonely terrapin the size of a dinner plate.

The terrapin ended up at Great Ayton RSPCA centre where we were filming at the time. I discovered that they can live in outside ponds and so volunteered ours as a home for Tony (named after the sound man). However, after finding out that terrapins bite ducks' feet I had to withdraw the offer. Later in my hotel room I told Mum about the adventures of Tony ending with the sad fact that he may have to be put to sleep. Terrapins are difficult to rehome as they can be vicious and carry salmonella.

'We can't let that happen!' Mum declared, and gave me the number of Jonathan Hodges' Wildlife Sanctuary in Staffordshire to see if they could help. Without hesitation they offered to take in Tony and find him a home. But the story didn't end there. I was going straight back to London and Mum and Dad couldn't leave home to come and collect Tony from me for another couple of days. My sister's spare bath solved the problem however and so that's where Tony and I headed for.

The RSPCA had put Tony in a small cardboard box on a wet towel but about half way through the train journey from Darlington to Kings Cross I feared that Tony may be getting dehydrated. I took him to the toilet and ran him under the tap but failed miserably in protecting Tony's privacy. As if sitting in the sink of a British Rail train toilet wasn't humiliating enough, Tony suffered that final insult when a lady opened the unlocked door and witnessed this unlikely scene. She took one look at Tony, screamed and ran off. You can find many strange things in British Rail toilets, but a king sized terrapin isn't usually one of them.

Tony's life got better however from then on. Anthea ran Tony's bath and sent her husband Peter out into the garden to dismantle part of the rockery. A major reconstruction of it took place in the bath and this was Tony's home for two days, until Mum and Dad collected him and took him to his new home in Staffordshire. Now he's safe and sound and does things that terrapins usually do, which is a far cry from his attempts at window shopping down Middlesbrough high street.

King-size terrapin taking a bath in a British Rail sink

Minced 'Beef' with Parsnip and Carrot Topping

A creative variation on cottage pie.

Serves four

40 mins

275g (10oz) *beef flavoured soya mince hydrated in 750ml (1¼ pints) of water. (Hydrate in the microwave for about 5 minutes or until tender). Soya mince may also be bought frozen and ready to use*
225g (8oz) *parsnips, peeled and chopped*
225g (8oz) *carrots, peeled and chopped*
1 *tablespoon of rapeseed oil*
1 *large Bramley cooking apple, peeled, cored and chopped*
2 *medium sized onions, peeled and sliced*
150ml (5 fl oz) *dry cider (we liked Merrydown Original Dry)*
1 *teaspoon of dried sage*
1 *pint of stock – Marmite stock cubes or vegetarian Oxo cubes*
25g (1oz) *soya margarine*

1. Boil the carrots and parsnips for about 15 minutes or until tender. Drain well, reserving the liquid for vegetable stock.
2. Mash with soya margarine until smooth, seasoning to taste. Keep hot.
3. Heat the oil in a roomy non-stick pan and fry the onions until tender and golden.
4. Add the apple and cook until tender.
5. Add the sage, soya mince and cider.
6. Add the stock.
7. Spoon the mixture into a suitable warm serving dish and spread the parsnip and carrot mixture on top.

'Bacon' and Parsley Pancakes

Although this takes time to prepare, the pancakes can be made in advance, while the 20 minutes cooking time allows plenty of time for pre-dinner drinks.

1 packet vegan rashers (available from your local healthfood shop) grilled or lightly fried then chopped into small pieces

Parsley Coating Sauce
2 level tablespoons of chopped parsley
20g (¾oz) cornflour
300ml (½ pint) soya milk
Small knob of soya margarine

Mustard 'butter'
50g (2oz) soya margarine and 1 level teaspoon of mustard creamed together

Basic Pancake Batter
100g (4oz) self-raising flour
250ml (½ pint) of soya milk
1 teaspoon of melted soya margarine
Whole egg replacer made up to the equivalent of one egg (check product for non animal content)

1. Sift the flour into a bowl.
2. Beat to a smooth batter with the egg replacer, melted margarine and half the milk.
3. Gradually add the rest of the milk.
4. Heat the margarine in a frying pan (20–20cm/ 8–9 inch pan) over a medium heat. When hot, pour in 2 to 3 tablespoons of the batter mixture, tilting the pan to cover. When golden brown toss or turn over and cook the other side.
5. To keep, put layers of greaseproof paper between the pancakes. Makes about 8 pancakes.
6. Make the parsley coating sauce – mixing the cornflour with a little cold milk taken from the half pint to make a smooth paste. Warm the remainder of the milk in a non-stick pan, then pour on the paste and mix well.
7. Heat and stir until the sauce boils and thickens.
8. Remove from the heat and add the margarine, then the chopped parsley.
9. Add the chopped 'bacon' rashers.
10. Spoon the mixture on to the pancakes and roll up. Place in an oven-proof dish.
11. Brush each pancake with a little mustard 'butter'.
12. Reheat in the centre of a moderate oven at 180°C (350°F) for 20 minutes or until thoroughly heated.

Serves four

50 mins + 20 mins

Mock Duck with Blackcurrant Conserve

My Mum shied away from Granose's Mock Duck for a long time. She feeds the ducks on the garden pond every day and to eat even a 'mock' one felt a little too close to home. I volunteered to try it out first and found that it is simply a variation on soya protein. It's incredibly tender and versatile and able to absorb different flavours to suit your particular taste. It's easy to cook with and I even know a meat eater or two who buy this product. Daffy and Donald can sleep easy.

Serves four

2 tins of Granose Mock Duck (available from your local health food shop)
2 heaped tablespoons of blackcurrant conserve
4 tablespoons of red wine (we used Cotes du Ventoux Rouge from Asda.)
1 tablespoon of green peppercorns
2 tablespoons of soy sauce
1 inch piece of fresh ginger
2 large cloves of garlic, crushed
2 red onions, finely chopped
Olive oil

1. Drain the Mock Duck reserving the liquid. Place in a shallow dish.
2. Pour 1 tablespoon of olive oil and the soy sauce over the duck and allow to stand whilst doing the following:
3. Heat 1 tablespoon of olive oil in a frying pan.
4. Add the piece of ginger and cook gently for two minutes allowing the ginger to flavour the oil. Remove the ginger piece and discard.
5. Add the garlic, the onions and half the green peppercorns and cook gently until soft.
6. Now add the Mock Duck plus the marinade and heat through.
7. In a small pan heat the blackcurrant conserve with the red wine and the remaining green peppercorns.
8. Remove the duck on to a warm plate, saving the pan juices and adding them to the blackcurrant conserve.
9. Pour the blackcurrant conserve over the Mock Duck and serve.

40 mins

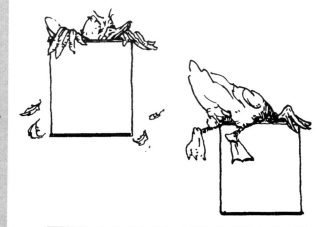

Mock Duck with Orange

2 cans of Granose Mock Duck, drained
    (available in your local health food
    shop)
2 tablespoons of rapeseed oil
1 heaped teaspoon of powdered ginger
700g (1½lb) onions, sliced
Juice and finely grated zest of 2 large
    oranges
2 tablespoons of Seville orange marmalade
1 large orange, thinly sliced
1 teaspoon of cornflour

1. Heat the oil and fry the onion and ginger for about 7 minutes or until the onion is tender.
2. Mix the orange juice, zest and marmalade together in a roomy non-stick pan on a low heat until the marmalade melts.
3. Transfer the Mock Duck, onion and ginger to the saucepan to marinate for half an hour.
4. Thicken the mixture using 1 teaspoon of cornflour (in a little water if necessary).
5. Microwave the slices of orange for 2 minutes or until tender, keeping their shape.
6. Put everything into a suitable casserole dish, cover and microwave until thoroughly hot. Alternatively, heat in a pre-heated oven at 190°C (375°F).

Serves four

40 mins

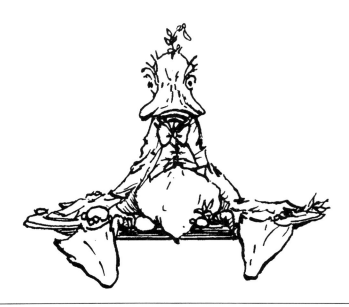

Fish Tales

We've all heard the 'I'm a vegetarian I only eat fish' routine. Why people think that land animals are a no-no but fish are fair game is beyond me; they suffocate to death and can struggle to live for several minutes before giving up the fight. In my book that's a pretty nasty way to die. However, 'vegetarian fish eaters' are commonplace and at least they're swimming in the right direction.

A little knowledge, though, can be a powerful thing, as I witnessed whilst filming on a salmon farm up in Scotland. Dan, the director of the piece, was one of the 'I'm a vegetarian I only eat fish' brigade and was rubbing his hands with glee at the thought of coming away with a succulent piece of salmon. The fish we were filming were extraordinarily energetic and kept leaping out of the water with a huge amount of speed and power. Were they trying to escape? Were they camera shy? Where they excited to see us? The farmer solved the mystery by informing us that they had lice, common, he said in salmon, and even though these fish are natural leapers, these were doing it higher and faster than usual in a vain attempt to get away from the itching.

The director didn't come away from that farm with any salmon and later on at dinner he chose the meat free option on the menu.

'Don't you want any lice flavoured salmon?' I teased.

'No,' he smiled bravely, 'Not tonight . . .'

Spicy 'Beef' Casserole

Soya chunks have a wonderful texture. You may find them in some supermarkets but more easily in your local health food shop. When hydrating always check that they are tender through to the middle.

275g (10oz) *beef flavoured soya chunks hydrated in 750ml (1¼ pints) of water. Hydrate in the microwave for about 15 minutes or until tender*
1 *tablespoon of rapeseed oil*
1 *teaspoon of ground coriander*
½ *teaspoon of ground cloves*
2 *teaspoons of ground cumin*
2 *cloves of garlic, crushed*
Juice of **2** *large oranges*
150ml (5fl oz) *Croft dry sherry (few sherries are vegan. Refer to the* Animal Free Shopper *to be sure!)*
75g (3oz) *no-soak apricots, chopped*
75g (3oz) *no-soak stoned prunes*
50g (2oz) *raisins*
2 *pints of stock – Marmite stock cubes or vegetarian stock cubes*

1. Place the hydrated chunks in a large non-stick pan. Add the orange juice, spices, rapeseed oil and garlic. Allow to marinate for about 1 hour.
2. Add the chopped apricots, prunes and raisins.
3. Put on a moderate heat and heat thoroughly. Add the sherry just before serving.

Serve with roast potatoes or vegetables of your choice.

Serves four to six

1 hour 10 mins

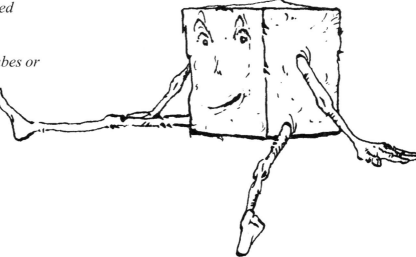

Pasta Bolognese Sauce

Balsamic vinegar and fresh basil make this vegan bolognese sauce rich and tasty

Sauce

4 medium onions, finely chopped
4 cloves of garlic, finely chopped
1 stick of celery, finely chopped
2 tablespoons of olive oil
1 level teaspoon of sugar
1 tablespoon of dried mixed herbs
2 tablespoons of fresh basil
2 tins of premium chopped tomatoes
2 tablespoons of balsamic vinegar
1 generous glass of red wine (we used Antica di Romanga Sangiovese from Safeway.)
A pinch of salt and pepper

Mince and mushrooms

225g (8oz) unflavoured soya mince hydrated in 600ml (1 pint) of water. (Hydrate in the microwave for about 5 minutes or until tender). Soya mince may also be bought frozen and ready to use.
125g (4oz) mushrooms, finely chopped

Pasta

400g (16oz) wheat pasta of your choice

1. Start by gently frying the onions, garlic and celery in olive oil in a non-stick pan on a low to moderate heat, then add all the rest of the sauce ingredients, stirring gently.
2. Turn the heat right down and leave to cook gently for about 20 minutes, stirring frequently.
3. Add the soya mince and mushrooms.
4. Turn up the heat and gently add a little more red wine if the mixture is too thick.
5. Cook gently for a further 10 minutes. Meanwhile, cook the pasta of your choice.
6. Serve together when the pasta is cooked through.

Toad in the Hole

Many of the vegetarian sausages on the market are not suitable for vegans because of their egg content. Read the list of ingredients on the various packets however and you will find some which are animal-free.

8 *vegan sausages (we used Linda McCartney's)*
Basic pancake batter

Basic Pancake Batter
100g (4oz) *self-raising flour*
250ml (½ pint) *soya milk*
1 *teaspoonful of melted soya margarine*
Whole egg replacer made up to the equivalent of one egg (check product for non-animal content)

1. Sift the flour into a bowl.
2. Beat to a smooth batter with the egg replacer, melted margarine and half of the milk.
3. Gradually add the rest of the milk.

To make the Toad in the Hole
1. Make up the basic pancake batter.
2. Arrange the sausages (defrost if frozen) in a 25cm × 30cm/10 in × 12in baking tin.
3. Bake just above the centre of a hot oven 220°C (450°F) for about 10 minutes or until cooked through.
4. Take out of the oven and pour in the basic pancake batter.
5. Bake for 30 minutes then reduce heat to 200°C (400°F) and bake for about another 15 minutes or until risen and golden brown.

Serves four

1 hour

Hot Dog

We used to have a lemon beagle hound called Tom. A small daughter of a friend of Mum's was round at the house one day and spotted the pale coloured Tom lying on the spare bed in the full sunlight.

'He's sunbathing!' Mum told her.

The little girl thought for a moment before asking, 'Will he turn brown?'

Desserts

Naughty But Nice!

Mum and Dad's dog, Toby, could chew for England. He only has to be left alone for the shortest space of time before seeking revenge by chewing someone's prize possession. My long suffering parents have returned home to find the entire contents of a wardrobe strewn about the house, belts and ties bitten in two, a settee ruined and every cushion in the house mauled to death.

It's been highly amusing watching Toby's antics from a distance, but not quite so amusing when he gets hold of something that belongs to you. One day, Mum, Dad and I returned home to find one of my vegetarian Dr Marten boots in tatters. This was obviously the final straw for my Mum. She cried, I swore and Dad tried to look on the bright side by producing the other boot and triumphantly declaring that it was perfectly intact. One Dr Marten boot, perfectly intact. Very useful. It has to be said that a local cobbler was able to perform some intricate and delicate surgery on the boot and render it wearable, and once again Toby was forgiven.

Apple & Sultana Strudel

The classic Teutonic dessert without the masses of dairy butter.

Serves four to six

450g (1lb) *eating apples, peeled, cored and sliced*
25g (1oz) *golden sultanas*
¼ teaspoon ground cinnamon
¼ teaspoon of mixed spice
1 250g (9oz) *packet of filo pastry, fresh or frozen*
Soya margarine

1. In a little water cook the apples gently on a low heat on the stove or microwave until just soft.
2. Add the sultanas, cinnamon and mixed spice without breaking up the apple slices.
3. Follow the direction for filo pastry on the packet, brushing with melted margarine. Work on a lightly greased large baking sheet, which is easier than trying to move the strudel on to it when filled!
4. Turn the apple mixture out on to the middle of the filo sheets, leaving a 5cm (2 inch) border on the short ends.
5. Fold the filo sheets over towards the middle to cover the filling and brush the top with the melted soya margarine.
6. Cook in a preheated oven at 200°C (400°F) for about 30 minutes or until crisp and golden.

Serve warm with soya cream or vegan ice cream.

1 hour

Summer Pudding

This exotic English *dessert is best made a day in advance of a dinner party, saving you hassle on the night.*

900g (2lb) *strawberries, raspberries, apples or any other fruit in season*
1 *packet vegetarian raspberry jelly crystals making 600ml (1 pint)*
1 *cinnamon stick*
2 *tablespoons of mixed spice*
6–7 *slices of white bread with crusts removed*

1. Line a 900g (2 pint) pudding basin with the bread, saving some for the top. Do not grease the basin.
2. Dissolve the jelly crystals and add the fruit and spices.
3. Gently simmer to soften the fruit. Remove the cinnamon stick.
4. Pour the mixture into the basin, setting about a cupful on one side.
5. Cover with bread. Put a saucer and a weight on top and place in the fridge for several hours until set, or overnight.
6. Dunk the basin in hot water to loosen the bread, then turn on to a plate.
7. Decorate with the reserved mixture.

Serve from the fridge with soya cream or vegan ice cream

Serves four to six

30 mins

47

Raspberry & Cherry Compote

An all year round fruity treat. Add fresh soft fruits when in season.

Serves four to six

1 290g can of raspberries in apple juice
1 420g can of red cherries in syrup
25g (1oz) cornflour

1. Drain off the juice from both cans to make about 300ml (½ pint).
2. Use a little to make a smooth paste with the cornflour.
3. Heat the rest of the juice in a non-stick pan and thicken with the cornflour, stirring all the time. Allow to cool but not set.
4. Arrange the fruit in a glass dish and pour the thickened juice over it. Refrigerate until set.

5 mins

Serve with soya cream or vegan ice cream

Unbeatable antidote to cold weather

Flaked Rice Pudding

Taking only minutes to prepare, this is a worthy animal-free version of the popular favourite. Topped with a blob of jam it is an unbeatable antidote to cold weather.

50g (12oz) *flaked rice*
25g (1oz) *sugar*
600ml (1 pint) *vanilla flavoured rice milk*
Nutmeg

1. Grease a 1 litre (1½ pint) pie dish with vegan margarine.
2. Put all the ingredients into the dish and sprinkle grated nutmeg on the top.
3. Bake in a pre-heated oven at 160°C (325°F) for about 1½ hours.

Serves four

1¾ hours

Spiced Bread & 'Butter' Pudding

Egg replacer works beautifully in this recipe. It's light and fluffy and you're sure to want seconds!

Serves four

5 slices of white bread spread with soya margarine
75g (3oz) golden sultanas
1 teaspoon of mixed spice
2 tablespoons of brown sugar
300ml (½ pint) soya milk
Whole egg replacer made up to equivalent of 1 egg (check product for non-animal content)

1. Grease a 1 litre (1½ pint) pie dish with soya margarine.
2. Place half the bread and margarine in the dish and sprinkle on the sultanas and half the sugar. Cover with the rest of the bread.
3. Whisk the egg replacer, milk and spice together and pour over the bread, letting it soak for 30 minutes.
4. Sprinkle the rest of the sugar over the top.
5. Bake in a pre-heated oven at 180°C (350°F) for about 1 hour.

1¾ hours Serve with soya cream.

Basic Shortcrust Recipe

225g (8oz) self-raising flour
125g (4oz) vegetable fat
Water to mix

1. Sieve the flour.
2. Add the fat and rub into the flour until the mixture looks like fine breadcrumbs.
3. Add enough water to form a dough.
4. Roll out on a floured surface.

If using Trex follow the recipe on the packet as the proportion of flour to fat is different i.e. 280g/10oz flour, 125g/4oz Trex.

Cherry Pancakes with Soya Cream

When in season, any soft fruits can be substituted for the cherry pie filling.

Basic Pancake Batter
100g (4oz) self-raising flour
250ml (½ pint) soya milk
1 teaspoon of melted soya margarine
Whole egg replacer made up to the
equivalent of one egg (check product
for non-animal content)

1. Sift the flour into a bowl.
2. Beat to a smooth batter with the egg replacer, melted margarine and half the milk.
3. Gradually add the rest of the milk.
4. Heat the soya margarine in the frying pan (20cm or 22cm / 8 inch or 9 inch pan) over a medium heat. When hot, pour in 2 to 3 tablespoons of the batter mixture, tilting the pan to cover. When golden brown toss or turn over and cook the other side.
5. To keep, put layers of greaseproof paper between the pancakes.

Makes about 8 pancakes

Filling
1 can of cherry pie filling
1 250ml carton soya cream

Spoon cherry pie filling on to half the pancake, add cream and fold.

51

Orange & Lemon Cheesecake

A special, rich, tangy dessert with an authentic full cream cheese taste.

Serves eight

Base
75g (3oz) soya margarine
40g (1½oz) brown sugar
75g (3oz) plain wholemeal flour
75g (3oz) fine porridge oats

1. Cream together the soya margarine and sugar.
2. Add the oats and flour and mix together thoroughly.
3. Press mixture into a greased, loose-bottomed 8 inch flan tin.
4. Bake in a pre-heated oven at 180°C (350°F) for 15 minutes until firm and browned.
5. Allow to cool then chill in the fridge while you make the topping.

Topping
225g (8oz) plain animal-free cream cheese
   (available from your local health
   food shop)
4 tablespoons of maple syrup
Rind of 1 orange, finely grated
Rind of 1 lemon, finely grated
Juice of 2 oranges
Juice of 1 lemon
2 teaspoons of Gelazone
2 tablespoons of mixed chopped nuts

1. Put the cream cheese, maple syrup, lemon and orange rind into a bowl and blend well.
2. Using a small pan, bring to the boil, on a moderate heat the Gelazone, orange and lemon juice.
3. Leave it to cool then pour into the cream cheese mixture and blend it all together, stirring occasionally.
4. When the mixture is almost at setting point pour it into the base. Leave in the fridge overnight to set firmly. Decorate with a generous covering of mixed chopped nuts.

1 hour

Healthy Apple Pie

Quick to make and sugar free! Try a blackberry and apple pie by using the apple pie recipe but with 450g/¾lb apples and 125g/¼lb fresh blackberries. Use the same proportions to make fruit pies such as rhubarb and apple and stoned plum and apple.

225g (8oz) *made or bought shortcrust pastry*
450g (1lb) *eating apples, peeled, cored and sliced*

1. Cook the apples with a little water on the stove top (or in a microwave oven) until just tender, but still whole pieces.
2. Grease a pie plate and line with half the pastry. Put the apples on the pastry and cover with the other half of the pastry.
3. Bake in a pre-heated oven at 230°C (450°F) for about 15 minutes or until the pastry is golden.

Serve with soya cream or vegan ice cream.

Serves eight

1 hour

Chocolate Cheesecake

Another decadent dessert that can be made a day ahead and served in an instant!

Serves eight

Base
100g (3½oz) *soya margarine*
450g (16oz) *digestive biscuits (check*
 product for non-animal content)

1. Gently melt the soya margarine in a saucepan.
2. Crush the biscuits until they resemble fine breadcrumbs.
3. Take the margarine off the heat and mix in the biscuit crumbs.
4. Press into a 28cm (11 inch) flan tin and chill in the fridge.

Topping
450g (16oz) *firm tofu, mashed*
Juice of 1½ oranges
Grated rind of 1 orange
55g (2oz) *cocoa powder*
55g (2oz) *soya margarine*
55g (2oz) *sugar*
2–4 tablespoons of soya milk
Orange or mandarin segments and
Vegan chocolate for decoration

1¼ hours

1. Using a food processor mix together the tofu, orange juice and rind, cocoa powder, margarine and sugar. Add the soya milk as necessary to ensure a smooth consistency.
2. Place the mixture over the base and smooth the top.
3. Cook for 35 minutes in a pre-heated oven at 180°C (350°F).
4. Allow to cool then chill in the fridge overnight.
5. Top this with slices of fresh orange or mandarin segments and finish off with a little grated vegan chocolate.

Baked Bananas with Rum

A tipsy, tropical temptation.

4 large ripe bananas
Grated rind and juice of 1 lemon
90g (3oz) soft brown sugar
1 level teaspoon of mixed spice
25g (1oz) soya margarine
3 tablespoons of rum

1. Peel the bananas and cut each in half lengthwise.
2. Using an oven-proof dish arrange them close together in a single layer.
3. Sprinkle the grated lemon rind over the top of the bananas then squeeze the juice over the top.
4. Mix together the sugar and spice and sprinkle evenly over the bananas.
5. Dot the margarine over the bananas.
6. Drizzle the rum over the bananas.
7. Cook in a pre-heated, moderate oven at 180°C (350°F) for 15 minutes or until the bananas are soft.

Serve hot with soya cream or dairy free ice cream available at all big supermarkets.

Serves four

25 mins

Peanut Butter Ice Cream Sundae with Chocolate Sauce

A quick and simple way to make vanilla ice cream deliciously extravagant. The sauce will keep in the fridge for up to three weeks if you leave out the soya cream until just prior to serving.

Serves four

15 mins

1 × 750ml (1¼ pint) *tub of vanilla soya ice cream*
150g (6oz) *crunchy peanut butter*

1. Using 4 bowls, spoon some of the ice cream into each one.
2. Cover with a level tablespoon of peanut butter.
3. Spoon a further layer of ice cream on top.
4. Cover with half a tablespoon of peanut butter.
5. Top with a final layer of ice cream.
6. Pour on the chocolate sauce.

Chocolate sauce
6 *tablespoons of carob powder*
6 *tablespoons of maple syrup*
6 *tablespoons of water*
6 *tablespoons of soya cream*

1. Put the carob powder, maple syrup and water into a small non-stick pan and heat gently over a low heat, stirring until well mixed. Remove from the heat.
2. When slightly cooled pour into a jug.
3. When cold add the soya cream.
4. Use immediately.

Nutty Apple Bake

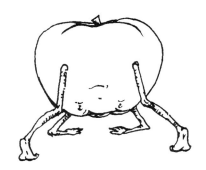

This 'upside down crumble' makes a nutty change — try it with rhubarb or pears.

Base
75g (3oz) mixed chopped nuts
4 level tablespoons of golden syrup
75g (3oz) soya margarine
150g (6oz) fine porridge oats

1. Place the golden syrup and margarine in a non-stick pan and melt over a low to moderate heat, stirring constantly.
2. Stir in the oats and nuts.
3. Spoon the mixture into a well-greased ¾ litre (1¼ pints) oven-proof dish and press the mixture down with the back of a spoon.

Topping
2 medium sized cooking apples, peeled, cored and sliced
2 tablespoons of caster sugar
1 level teaspoon of cinnamon
25g (1oz) soya margarine

1. Arrange the apples over the base.
2. Mix together the sugar and cinnamon and sprinkle over the apples.
3. Put small knobs of margarine over the apples.
4. Bake in a pre-heated oven at 180°C (350°F) for about 45 minutes.

Serve hot with soya cream or dairy-free ice cream available at all big supermarkets.

Serves eight

1 hour

Cakes and Biscuits

Sweet Revenge

Room service menus can be great fun for the animal-free eater. Vegetarian options are almost always not suitable for vegans and so it's down to you to make up your own dish. On the whole, chef usually takes your request in his stride as you explain to him that you really *will* enjoy a banana and avocado sandwich without butter. There are few things more frustrating however than working out some weird and wonderful concoction at 11.10 p.m. only to discover that the room service ends at 11 p.m. sharp.

One night I arrived at a hotel in San Antonio, Texas and had that very problem. A combination of unappetising airline food and jet lag resulted in a state of near starvation by 4 a.m. The in-room coffee making facility went some way to relieving the situation but even a nibble of the rose scented bathroom soap began to look like a tempting proposition. How could I film our story about chimps the next day if I was weak through lack of nourishment? Unable to sleep I read and re-read the room service menu that would not be available for another three hours at the first serving of breakfast. I could stand this torture no longer and put the menu back on the bedside table, only to make the grim discovery that I was not the only person to have slept in that bed suffering the agony of extreme hunger. The occupant before me had forgone the temptation of the rose scented soap and opted for his own nails instead. Unable to swallow them however, he had contented himself with a good old chew before discarding each nail in turn on the carpet by the bed.

Now, how often do we British dare to complain about anything? So what if you're paying for a room which hasn't been cleaned properly since the place opened? Well this time was different and flinging British reserve to one side I gathered up the offending nails and strode down to reception to make my displeasure known. Scattering the nails over the desk and demanding to see the manager seemed to do the trick and I accepted the 'superior king size jacuzzi room' with a great deal of smug satisfaction. But I wasn't smiling for long. The jacuzzi jets didn't only spurt out water but cockroaches too! As I flushed the already dead creatures down the toilet I concluded that this was the hotel's subtle way of taking revenge for all those nails I scattered over their reception. It also occurred to me that whilst swanning off abroad to film with potentially dangerous animals, it's always the creepy crawlies you meet along the way that test your nerve the most.

Ginger Spice Loaf

An ideal accompaniment for afternoon tea, or simply as a sweet and spicy snack.

Serves eight

225g (8oz) white self-raising flour, sifted
50g (2oz) soft brown sugar
1 rounded teaspoon of baking powder
1 rounded teaspoon of ground ginger
1 rounded teaspoon of mixed spice
2 heaped tablespoons of black treacle
150ml (¼ pint) soya milk

1. Put the milk and treacle into a non-stick pan and mix together on a very low heat until well blended.
2. Put the flour, spices and baking powder into a bowl. Add the sugar.
3. Make a well in the middle and pour in the treacle and milk mixture. Stir in well.
4. Pour into a greased and line 454g (1 lb) loaf tin.
5. Bake on a shelf below the centre of a pre-heated oven at 180°C (350°F) for about 40 minutes or until a thin knife put into the centre comes out clean.
6. Turn out onto a cooling rack.
7. Leave a day before slicing.

1 hour

Spread with soya margarine to serve.

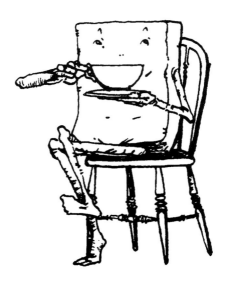

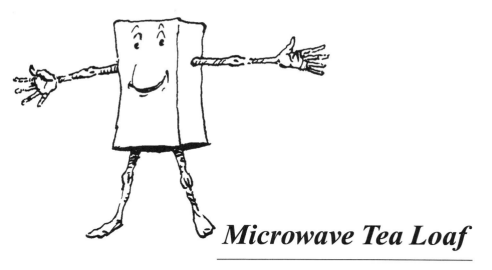

Microwave Tea Loaf

Amazingly quick, easy and delicious!

300g (10oz) *mixed sultanas, raisins and*
    chopped cherries
200ml (8fl oz) *strong tea*
125g (4oz) *carob 'chocolate'*
175g (6oz) *self-raising flour*
1 *banana, well mashed*

1. In a bowl suitable for the microwave, mix together the fruit and the tea. Cook on 're-heat' for 7 minutes.
2. Break up the carob 'chocolate' into small pieces and stir into the mixture until it has melted.
3. Working quickly, beat the sugar, flour and banana.
4. Spoon the mixture into a suitable microwave cake dish. Place in the microwave on an upturned plate and cook on 'high' for 7 minutes. If your microwave plate does not rotate automatically then rotate by hand every 2 minutes.
5. Allow the cake to stand for 5 minutes.
6. Turn out onto a cooling rack.

Spread with soya margarine to serve.

Serves
eight

30 mins

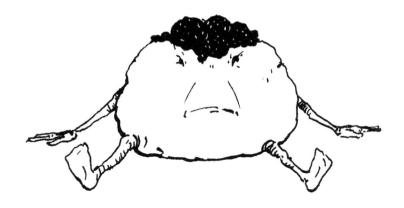

Strawberry Buns

Substitute raspberry jam for strawberry jam or any other suitable jam of your choice, e.g. apricot or blackcurrant.

Serves six to eight

30 mins

225g (8oz) wholemeal flour
1½ teaspoons of baking powder
25g (1oz) soya margarine
25g (1oz) caster sugar
150ml (¼ pint) soya milk
4 tablespoons of strawberry jam

1. Sift the flour and baking powder into a bowl.
2. Rub in the soya margarine until the mixture resembles fine breadcrumbs.
3. Add the sugar then all the soya milk and mix into a dough.
4. Knead the dough on a lightly floured board until it is smooth.
5. Roll into 6–8 balls and place them on a greased baking tray well apart.
6. Make little holes in the centre of each bun and fill with the jam.
7. Bake in a pre-heated oven at 200°C (400°F) for about 12–15 minutes until risen and slightly browned.

American Survival Bars

Packed with goodness, these are a great animal-free alternative to chocolate bars.

2¼ cups of dry porridge oats **325g (12oz)**
1½ cups of puffed wheat or similar **25g (1oz)**
4½ cups of Kelloggs Ricicles **125g (4oz)**
¾ cup of wheat bran **125g (4oz)**
¾ cup of concentrated apple or orange
    juice **175ml (6fl oz)**
3 tablespoons of date syrup
3 tablespoons of black molasses
¾ cup of mixed raisins and sultanas **75g (3oz)**
50g (2oz) no-soak apricots, finely chopped
50g (2oz) cherries, finely chopped
1 teaspoon of ground cinnamon

1. Put all the ingredients together in a large bowl and mix thoroughly.
2. Pour into a 25cm × 25cm/10 in × 10 in greased tin and flatten.
3. Bake for about 50 minutes in a pre-heated oven at 135°C (275°F).
4. Cut into required shapes while still warm.
5. Leave in the tray to cool.

Serves eight

1 hour

Sweet & Savoury Scones

Where would we be without the trusty and versatile scone? You can add to the basic recipe to create endless sweet and savoury variations, some of my favourites are below.

Makes ten

15 mins + 10 mins

Basic Scones
225g (8oz) *self-raising flour*
50g (2oz) *soya margarine*
125ml (¼ pint) *soya milk*

Savoury Scones

Parsley Scones
Add 1 teaspoon of finely chopped fresh parsley before adding the milk

Herb Scones
Add 1 teaspoon of dried herbs before adding the milk.

Sweet Scones

Spiced Scones
Add **25g (1oz)** *of caster sugar and 1 teaspoon of cinnamon or mixed spice before adding the milk.*

Fruit Scones
Add **25g (1oz)** *of caster sugar and* **50g (2oz)** *of mixed dried fruit before adding the milk. If preferred, substitute the dried fruit for sultanas or cherries or currants.*

1. Sift the flour into a bowl and rub in the soya margarine until the mixture resembles fine breadcrumbs.
2. Make a well in the middle and add the milk. Mix into a soft dough.
3. Working quickly, turn out onto a floured board and knead until smooth.
4. Roll out to about 1cm (¼ inch) thickness
5. Cut out into rounds with a 6cm (2½ inch) biscuit cutter. Transfer to a greased baking tray.
6. Bake in a pre-heated oven at 230°C (450°F) towards the top. Bake for about 8–10 minutes until risen and golden.
7. Cool on a wire rack.

Makes about 10 scones

Cherry Carob Cookies

Colourful cookies with a hint of carob.

100g (4oz) *plain flour, sifted*
100g (4oz) *soya margarine*
50g (2oz) *caster sugar*
½ teaspoon of vanilla essence
25g (1oz) *carob chocolate, coarsely grated*
25g (1oz) *green glacé cherries, chopped finely*

1. Cream the soya margarine and sugar together and add the vanilla essence.
2. Add the cherries and carob chocolate.
3. Stir in the flour.
4. Put 20 teaspoons of the mixture (well apart as the mixture will spread) on a greased baking tray.
5. Bake just above the centre of a pre-heated oven at 190°C (375°F) for 15 to 20 minutes.
6. Leave on the baking tray for a few minutes before transferring to a cooling rack.

Makes twenty

30 mins

Index of ingredients